A DRINK AT THE MIRAGE

PRINCETON SERIES OF CONTEMPORARY POETS

For Other Books in the Series,
see page 66

A DRINK
AT THE MIRAGE

MICHAEL J. ROSEN

PRINCETON UNIVERSITY PRESS

Copyright © 1984 by Princeton University Press
Published by Princeton University Press, 41 William Street,
Princeton, New Jersey 08540
In the United Kingdom: Princeton University Press, Guildford, Surrey

All Rights Reserved

Library of Congress Cataloging in Publication Data will be
found on the last printed page of this book

ISBN 0-691-06627-2
ISBN 0-691-0147-5 (pbk.)

Publication of this book has been aided by a grant from the Paul Mellon Fund
of Princeton University Press

Clothbound editions of Princeton University Press books are printed on acid-free
paper, and binding materials are chosen for strength and durability. Paper-
backs, although satisfactory for personal collections, are not usually suitable for
library rebinding

Printed in the United States of America by Princeton University Press
Princeton, New Jersey

ACKNOWLEDGMENTS

*Acknowledgment is gratefully made to the following
publications in which these poems have previously appeared:*

"Total Eclipse," *The Atlantic*

"The Fire Pond," *The New Yorker*

"The Woman in Ice," "Calling into Question,"
   The Carolina Quarterly

"The Age When Parents Don't Need Reasons," "Blind Minotaur
   Guided by a Little Girl in the Night," "Next," "Strand,"
   The Nation

"Hidden Pictures," *The New England Review*

"Roadside Sanctuary," "In Central Park" (under the title,
   "Provided with 'Perhaps'"), "What's Wrong with this
   Picture?," "Pony Penning Day" (under the title "Nowhere
   but Older"), *Shenandoah*

"Story Problem," *The Seattle Review*

"November," "November Again," *The Agni Review*

"Precipitation," "Notes through the Winter," *Columbia:
   a Magazine of Poetry and Prose*

"The Cutting of Nijinsky's Feet," *The Poetry Review*

"At Brunch We Entertain the Notion of the Perfect Place
   to Live," *Michigan Quarterly Review*

*I would like to thank the Ingram Merrill Foundation and the
Ohio Arts Council for support while writing many of these
poems; and Mimi Brodsky Chenfeld, Miriam Flock, and
Mark Svede for that fixity of attention known alternately as
criticism and love.*

CONTENTS

A DRINK AT THE MIRAGE

When the water-holes went dry people sought to drink at the mirage.
— Evelyn Waugh

Pony Penning Day

Older ponies recognize the men
and wade the swamps and marshland
to the bay where the boats are waiting.
Above the surf the crowd
on Chincoteague can hear the firemen
prodding the ponies to swim,

the rumbling of their voices cupped
among the oncoming waves.
The channel isn't wide; none have drowned
in crossing, though half were lost
once in a squall and stranded along
Virginia, stiff as wooden toys

standing on their sides or upside down,
the way a boy would leave them,
deciding on a swim. The long poles
push the ponies bobbing up
and down in a carrousel of waves,
toward the shallows. On the shore

they seem too heavy to swim,
to hold their weight, or ours—or hollow.
The herd parades down the road
the tourists line, as though returning
from some Homeric voyage,
years at sea, islands away from home.

All afternoon the ponies
are led on and off the platform
in a line it seems years won't exhaust.
The children pick out patterns
they like, while the fathers bid on ones
which look easier to break.

Sunday the firemen swim the unsold
across the sound to Assateague
where tiretracks and footprints mark the beach
from Thursday. There the ponies
lie down and kick and roll in the sand:
not happy nor unhappy,

not mourning like Achilleus' horses,
nor like Achilleus himself
drowning his tears in the dust, but soaked
and so must dry their coats,
mortal among mortal men, without
gods to mete their fates, or trust.

The Cutting of Nijinsky's Feet

What they wanted were the feet.
Not the cranium-size, weight of the soul,
or some canker of madness. Not the kidneys
that burst. Finally heavy as stones,
the feet at rest on a metal table,
they analyze the camber of the point,
the high arches, the tendon's strength.
They ink the soles and stamp a dozen prints.
Rotating joints, they plot the turn-out
and tensions from first through fifth position.
The callouses so thin, the toes firm as pink buds,
the scalpel unfurls each layer, the skin blooms red.
Cuneiform, navicular, cuboid, calcaneus,
the bones are delivered white and occult as eggs.
Tarsus, metatarsals, digits, one through five,
the bones are passed from hand to hand, examined
like dice, for marks or some notching of fate.
But they find nothing rare: not one bone
riddled with air sacs, not a vestige
of Hermes' talaria fixed at the ankle,
not the blood dripped in petals on the table.
Before the funeral the bones are sewn in place,
and after, Beaumont, from the Mariinsky confessed,
The weight of the coffin was almost intolerable.
That reminds me of what my ballet teacher has printed,
Gravity is the root of all lightness.
across the studio mirrors where we position ourselves,
our bodies like nothing we want.

Ice Sculptures

If the hotel were tall enough to reach
another climate, they could be icicles,
broken from a story where cold succeeds
itself for days — like days.
Too late to be out walking, you can witness
something locked between the sous chefs' arms,
hugged against their bodies like a child
afraid to sleep alone, but left
beside the backdoor, a foundling.
Sometimes you can recognize the animal
caught in the ice, actual-size,
already softened from the spotlights:

a teardrop swan, its neck looped
backward like a shoelace, an owl
or some pear-shape with rounded eyes,
a deer with long forelegs like paper clips,
a dolphin straddling the damp sidewalk,
and once, a curled thing, a child, in fact,
asleep, covered with curls, and horned—
as if, at the last moment, the chef decided
to carve a ram. Another night,
to prove that no one needs a metaphor:
a broken snow goose, draining red sauce
across the concrete down to where the bus stops.

The commas tooled in rows of curls,
the patterned chips of fur and pin feathers,
ribbing stripes, crosshatched scales:
all these evaporate before the last seating
as though the soul had lived in those details.
Now, no longer wanted, they wait
between the trashbins with the strays,
whatever they were, forgotten
like the cats' names—completely clear
or colorless, the silver of the mirror back
or the colors of whomever looks there
should someone bend that close.

6

Last winter, two weeks below freezing,
they mounted in a pyramid
(the garbage men never took them,
whether they tried or weren't required)
assembling a hecatomb of animals
which did nothing to appease the cold.
Tails sprouted claws which bore hooves
cleaved to tongues—another torso
grew haunches—fleshed with wings—imped
with antlered heads and fins: every beast
you could remember was preserved in ice
until the weather broke and they were loosed again.

The Woman in Ice

for my father

The balloon that I was holding read:
WOMAN IN ICE AT DON'S USED CARS.
You bought me cider and wandered through the lot.
It started drizzling. In the circus tent
lay an ice block the size of coffins
with a woman inside, all naked skin
except a two-piece swimming suit and cap,
mouthing, *Hello, hello.* She had promised
to stay encased till every car was sold
and her knees and shoulders surfaced
like islands after ages of melting.
It *was* melting; I straddled the mud
to tap above her blurry face, *Are you cold?*
and hugged my arms pretending to be chilled.
Her bluish smile shaped the same two circles,
Hello, hello. I asked again, *Are you cold?*
and tried to clear the frost with your keys
when a man much older than you, a man
I didn't know, took me in his arm
and carried me—crying, to each umbrella
until I found you. At home your voice
hovered close above me and you vouchsafed
the secret device of dummy legs and mirrors
and how the whole time she was warm as cider.
If it was easy then to sleep, falling
as your voice grew distant, I never dreamed
your face was ghosted in the block of ice
or that a secret, when repeated, starts to age.

Roadside Statuary

Imagine the surprise: bushels of sun-
burnt peaches under the day's clouded sky,
and then, behind the fruit shed, a whole kingdom
cast from the same grey firmament,
all facing forward, as though leaving home.

Squirrel, Swallowtail, Swan, a train of Ducks
(all waiting for St. Francis?), all frail things
with one exception: the already armored
Armadillo, made stonier in stone.
Names, not animals, are assembled here,
rows identical even to a bird's eye,
straight as soldiers, even soldier's tombs—
nearly grave, and yet commemorating
nothing, like zeros, but the place they hold.

Perhaps it's beauty they exemplify—
an idea so precious it can weather
such stand-ins for stone as concrete or clay.
Perhaps the beauty will spring up around them:
a garden where toads like these would look real?

Examples are provided: a grotto,
two wheelbarrows burdened with impatiens,
and everywhere, fountains with actual coins,
adorations of petunias, peeping frogs
(those toads, of course, kneedeep in lily pads),
caryatids, columns in perfect ruin,
and women, each titled rather than named,
who bear bouquets of water, conches that brim
with water, hands cupped—even broken hands.

Diana, shoots a steady stream of arrows,
Rebecca, waits beside a well, near *Joan,*
whose shield is forged of water. The mermaid's

ringing mist has sprayed a faint mandorla
behind the Virgins, arms wide without grief.

And here, well worth the wait, St. Francis, cast
in ageless speech with flocks of the unmoved:
lifesize with at least ten attentive pigeons,
child-size with pigeons for his playmates and toys,
and then a pigeon-size St. Francis, listening
at our feet. At last, something remotely real
surrounds us: pigeons, all grey, clouded
with grey, like pieces of a fallen sky.
Not one of them is startled by our approach.

In Central Park

Perhaps the truth depends on a walk around a lake.
—Wallace Stevens

There, across the reservoir, are suggestions of
trees, or reminders, non-specific, not
palmate or pinnate—the kind drawn on flash-cards
where the new word TREE is boldface on the back.
Forest-, true-, and *ever-green* identify
the three common flora of the genus *Far*
which circle the water *(sea-green* means water):
the trees are propped up with the stiff folding flaps
that stand the framed snapshots of the family.

Behind, in the taller second and third tiers,
the skyscrapers overlap, all of them grey,
several shades: some are obviously older,
almost phantoms, others are so faint they seem
forgotten in the background. Eventually
one will evaporate into the grey clouds
placed above them (in the *sky-blue* that means sky).
On the lake, the brightly colored dots mean birds,
fifty to one hundred fifty, one flock,

though the same dots, fixed in different positions,
mean raindrops, petals for late-spring tulips
or big stenciled snowflakes for a winter scene.
But while I am walking the circular walk
not a single bird flies down or flies away,
the dots don't flap their wings, dive — even drift.
Where they float, time has been fixed: the center where
the watch-hands attach and have nothing to tell.
The mesh fence enclosing the lake means

crumbs bring them no nearer—they can't be *pigeons*—
and stones fall short, however far they are thrown.
There is nowhere closer wherever I stand.
What are they? *snowgeese? seagulls? ducks?* or *decoys?*
They are waterbirds, at any rate, bird-like,
a kindred idea which seems in keeping.
The scene is finished. But then, it never fails:
someone running always stops to ask the time,
and truth is, someone really means the time.

Spectacles: A Late Spring

Backwards and backlit in red,
the word, W O N D E R, enlightens
the city like a new theme
to be copied from the blackboard
and printed in our notebooks.

The view from here (our *outlook*
you might say) though rose-
colored and near-sighted,
is the all-night supermart;
urchins huddled around the new

blood-pressure machine,
(a quarter tells them how young
and healthy and bored they are);
and a closed-off courtyard of trees
holding back the green,

holding the weather against us.
Yet the sign repeats its lesson—
Will we ever get it right?—
with no more impatience than the moon,
lending its already borrowed sunlight.

The other word, B R E A D,
is held (not hostage, really)
among the rows of houses
which the city raffles
for a dollar: vacant, except

for bulbs that someone planted,
forcing their old way to light.
Next, in the leftover glow
from the Donut Hole, a building
which abandons year-long dreams

of profit or nonprofit
bears a lone slogan, painted
pale brick-red on bricks:
D O I N G   O N E   T H I N G   W E L L.
Either the stone is still absorbing

the words or just revealing them
to drivers caught at the traffic light
an easy eye-chart distance away.
Though most never see the sign
even the one who does has little time

to think of what it meant and to whom
before the light changes
and in the rear-view mirror
the next car back, already late,
is shouting, *Green! It's green!*

At Brunch
We Entertain the Notion
of the Perfect Place to Live

As though it were childhood itself, you suggest
each place your family moved: not countries, but vast
pronunciations—a makeshift map would help. "Look,
we are *here*, the President McKinley matchbook;
this archipelago of pumpernickel crumbs:
the Azores; our Perrier bottle with spider mums
(already posing as a *vase*) can stand for Guam;
the pepper shaker, the sugar packets: Taiwan,
Corsica, Corfu, the Philippines..." I'm confused,
lost in these latitudes, the lassitude
drawn out between our Poles. It's already four? At last
the waiter clears off the tabletop and Atlas-
like, shoulders our worldly views and walks out scoffing.
Nice, Caracas, Turin, Fez—all lost in the offing!

Outside a Milton Avery Exhibit

Here are the colors we would paint our lives,
given a sable brush minute enough
for all the unforeseen, painstaking
details of how every day is numbered.

These are, no less, the colors we dream in:
aquamarine, dark wine, salmon and *sand,*
values named for things more live than color
which fade as dreams must, handed down from sleep.

These same horizons, painted within our reach,
complete a world seceded from our own—
if only we'd stand still for that, or sleep.
Instead we watch outside the curtainless, canvas-

size window. Below, a long construction-
paper chain of men has separated into
details: bricklayers, masons, carpenters,
each daubed with tangerine hard hats and stood

among the pick-up sticks, puzzles, and blocks,
like so many playthings someone could have spilled
from here: eighteen floors—they might as well be years—
above the all-too-soon-to-be-completed site.

ARTIST'S PROOF

Total Eclipse

The night of the eclipse we're parallel
in the unprecedented heat, secured
by just our fingers' intersecting touch.
Like the magician's other hand, the heat

distracts us while the moon vanishes
into the same black silk that conjures doves.
Making light of the heat, of anything
but the heat, we forget we meant to be up,

squinting to draw the moon into our lashes,
remarking how the blinds have magnified
the moon into a bright pinpoint of heat—
the moon! already half shadowed, half lit

on the window screen like a lunar moth.
So heavy-lidded, first one, then the other
detects some change: a quarter less, five-
eighths, or maybe still two halves....

we gaze until the moth closes its wings
and the same remaining crescent glistens
on your cheekbone, shoulder, hip—asleep
in a universe just outside my arms.

At 2:38, the scheduled fullest phase,
I wake you, once, though whether or not
you see the nothing that is there to see
—all overlapping shadows—I let you sleep.

For one held moment, the yielded space between us,
the unable-to-be-reasoned space beyond,
the sun and earth, my body, yours, the moon,
are all aligned in the predicted dark.

Next

In Puvis de Chavannes, the figures posed
along the landscape are other landscapes,
places we have been or mean to be

(though their combined horizon stretches farther
than a man can see at one time—or in one lifetime).
The amphora poised on the slenderest shoulder

is how everything is balanced: the sky
supported by the columns of trees, the earth
suspended from their shade, and between the two,

an overall lavender and well-kept greenery.
No one can move without the river overflowing
or the pear dropping from the baby's reach.

Even we must stand this far away,
squinting from the other side of the stream
or into the stream itself. What do we see

reflected if not ourselves, posed there
a moment, before moving to the next?

Another Figurescape

Clear water, a solid treeline, eight clouds
an arm's length of blue apart, who could identify
this place, as in each survey course,
label its period and probable artist?

Sunlight casts the naked body as it always has.
Classical, Neoclassical—even Abstraction
claims what hasn't changed: by the flat stones
a cluster of youths laugh and oil each other

while one, ankle deep in surf, rehearses
a *contra posto* stance: akimbo first,
then shifting hips, arms overhead,
he models a body that was beautiful

before anyone had drawn it from the landscape.
You take his offer, sketching the forms
he takes, perhaps gives, scaling the wells
his collar bones shape, the notch between

where a thumb will fit: topography, exotic
as any coastline where we dream of setting foot.
Like the furrowed beach, even the swells of muscle
on his stomach insist the current has produced them:

a body no less mythical than any other beast,
than your own body to me, than my own.
And yet the more you watch, the more I recognize
the light you see by is the light I love.

Like a breath of air (Why even call it *inspiration?*),
your near body fills those fallible lines.
You are the subject whatever you draw from,
wherever the weight is shifted or displaced.

"Blind Minotaur Guided by a Little Girl in the Night"

an etching by Picasso

The night is neither inhospitable
nor holy, with stars distributed, not in signs,
not crosses so much as the crosses crossed out,
as if the constellations were a chart
of our corrections: all we wished to believe.

Outside the myth the minotaur is blind.
The maze was all he saw: a fleet arrived,
the youths and virgins knew the way inside,
and knew there was none out. The whole exchange
took place on faith, *was* faith—no need to see.

Still the minotaur gazes at the sky.
What he cannot see is what the little girl can:
darkness or simply nothing, fabled with stars.
But the barefoot child is looking back
—apparently that's not forbidden here.

It seems the past is all she guides him toward,
his own story she could read out loud each night.
Her hair is just as delicate as the dove
nested in her arms. Maybe it will bring
a sign from where they're bound, or where they've been:

something green enough for hope. Later
it may cross the sky and reappear, a star.
Certainly she's young enough to wish.
The others present are unobserved, as yet:
a boatswain gathering a weathered net

with proof of where he's been, a gondolier
whose slender pole will guide him safely home,
and someone else, considering all this,
chin in one hand, elbow in the other,
(a poet, no doubt) distributing the stars

into a bird, a bull of sorts, a child—
children always piloted the blind.

Artist's Proof

During the sitting, sunlight had composed
a ladder out of nowhere—out of dust,
really, but it led nowhere, as though to mock
our conversation: one of those endlessly
inviting talks where *someday soon* sounds
like tomorrow, and *our sixth month, Friday,*
sounds scant for all this ease.

Except for that one stretch of sun, the air
has been three hours thinned with violet grey;
nothing to expose the brown of last year's lawn,
the ember of a cardinal flitting on the fire escape,
or—it was the shade that darkened your eyes—
the image of someone else who modeled here,
more laughing than holding still.

If I search, the studio provides belongings
from that time: the fan we fall asleep by,
a partly varnished desk—where one object
is missing another reminds you of it:
the borrowed books...the books with brief inscriptions...
words you can't take back. Call them posterns
to the other side of choice

usually no more distracting than the breath
that comes between words. Yet on the first
cold morning in October, speech condenses—
a door opens and the other choice appears...
in a crowd, for instance, after a matinee,
when our teary eyes aren't yet adjusted to light
and we catch ourselves discussing

the comparatively little we've endured.
We do adjust. We keep from harm by keeping
what harmed us once: fan, desk, your mistaken
eyes; forgetting is a more exact remembering,
where to place what can't be overlooked.
Call them portraits, half-finished, yes,
but wholly remembered (rote

as your address at six years old, that ends:
"...North America, America, earth, the Milky Way,
and whatever comes after that"). The first hangs
on the wall of a second, in the background, abstracted,
of a third...attic of a fourth...joke of a fifth.
The faces lose expression, features, and in time
they're indistinguishable

from each other, and the trees this side of vanishing.
On the other side of vanishing are other paintings,
other painters with their own perspectives.
Say the horizon is a time-line, then what I see
looking past you is *now,* simply these
however many choices in a composition
where twelve peonies

tolling below the window sill, are naples
yellow, glazed red violet red.
They will not show the fear that these months
beside you won't find six more; they do not mean
you are merely the choice above others or details
gathered from those I kept replacing like buds
in one implausible still life.

Even though I paint your reflection, your refraction,
I do not recognize you anywhere
but in this one portrait (can I call it *one?*)
that leads—like that illusion of a ladder—
from painted-over canvas to canvas yet-
to-paint, all of them *after* you, already
assuming you have gone.

If I could stipulate, *of a harmless nature,*
each sitting is a kind of accident:
one witness retelling what happened, the next one
lying, the one after swearing it's true.
We listen to them as we've listened to each other:
both sides prolonging this incident of light
with figures, no longer incidental.

Primitive Examples

Salt

The lone relief is propped among the monotony
of shelves: a town beseiged by salt, crystals
tamped into the impasto drifts.
Twelve houses straddle the glistening road
like giant footprints this artisan made, sowing
the coarse salt along the walks. Impossibly
instead of melting, the snow has been preserved.
This snowy scene resembles other scenes
before it resembles snow. The well-spaced trees
continue a border from artist to artist,
from quilted coverlet to stenciled chest.
Here is a world of countable objects, each thing
set worlds apart, and next to one another.
Even shadows repeat their humble subjects.

Glitter

Lost in a mountainous robe, a mother and child
are poised on a base with serrated blades of grass.
A good two-thirds, what remains is purest
backdrop: the last of the alchemies
of gold (already gone from solid to leaf
to foil and now to glitter). This latest fool's
gold—the ore of an artist's faith—is shaken
from a bottle and pasted in place. It signals
that lambent other empire, worthless as the mirror's
silver without the colors of this world:
A sky-blue, but where is a sky? a raiment
painted the white of something still to paint...
pigments squeezed from the tube, as though blending
were discontent; thinning, a lack of faith.

Chewing Gum

Near those works, and (now) moved from the window
a plywood angel leans at an awkward
backward tilt, above a handful of tempera-
splashed pebbles, his lowly firmament.
As August burned on and on, the room possessed
an unaccountable scent of peppermint.
No one once accused the carving (its apt
ingenuous device, yet undiscovered)
until, in the heat, losing its balance, it fell
from the pedestal. Unbelievably
we found the angel, bare feet embedded
firmly in the Kirman rug, still guyed
by one abiding line, one ductile thread
of evidence making the connection.

MAKING SCENES

Hidden Pictures

*A child's game of finding objects camouflaged inside
a larger picture.*

Here the teacup is drawn
in the sleeping hand: fingertips
have formed the rim, the volar well,
one finger unfurled for the handle,
as if another hand had held it
to the lips, drank half,
dressed, and hurried off to work.

The letter *P* follows the waves
that fill the pad beside the phone.
Someone familiar with the hand
will find a list of errands, a note
to call me when you wake, and know
the paraph stands for *Philip* or for *Paul.*

On the dresser the clock is drawn
in the watermark a glass has made.
He guesses the time and if he's alone.
If he calls *Philip?* or *Paul?*
and no one answers, the question will hang
till he comes home. Among the jonquils
bought the week before, he finds
a question mark curled, and wonders
if it was an exclamation
point that wilted, left unsaid.
He could be wrong about the time.

The other pillow is a dozing cat.
He imagines anything
he doesn't like, feline, found
asleep like that, waiting like strays
to be taken in and named.
P wants cats about, posing

along the sill and the sofa back.
He pulls the covers over the pillow.
All day he knows the cat
is sleeping in that one position.

As if to climb from bed, a ladder
shimmers along the pattern of light
shining through the leaded panes.
Perhaps first thing in the morning
a bulb would be replaced, something
painted, or taken down. He follows
his shadow climbing the rungs as he rises,
imagining there is someone else
outside, painting on a ladder
and here is his shadow at work since eight.

His robe is folded in a square
neater than he would have left it.
In the mirror he sees the morning sky:
it looks like rain. He decides rain
or not, he'll stay inside,
make coffee, cook, clean,
get some reading done, leave
nothing to imagination.
That is the order of the day.

He finds a list of things
to do that won't accomplish more
than leading room to room. He finds
himself alone and cannot see it
otherwise, the morning light
depressing, his voice a surprise at three:
no one was called, called, or came by.
If nothing else he could have dressed.

At five the recipes dictate
his time: *one hour to thaw the veal,
reduce the sauce, snip the dill,
puree the soup. P* will come home

late or soaking wet, bringing
the wine that won't be chilled as yet.
But everything will fall in place:
the table is set, linen, flowers,
the dinner served the way he likes it,
course after course, the day cleared
of papers and all the things he found
he couldn't hide or just forget.

What's Wrong With This Picture?

A child's game of finding errors concealed inside a larger picture.

for Miriam Flock

Six o'clock...the numbers read
correctly, clockwise...there is weather
out the window, clouds mostly,
an outline of a sunset with colors
easily imagined...a dining room,
a couple seated, dinner on the table...
the flatware matches, properly set,
the pepper shaker has three holes,
there's water inside the vase
of four five-petaled flowers—
no, one with four—and a fifth
petal half-hidden by the salt.

Perhaps what's wrong is that their lives
are set with such precise arrangements.
Maybe the pictures by the breakfront...
a shadow of bushes facing the sun?
a lattice with one slat misplaced?
or the phone? a thin directory
of friends to call, other couples
who might join them later for coffee...
so far, no sign of what's missing,
no ullage in the wine glass to read
either way. If anything's wanting
perhaps what's wrong is just to want it.

Maybe a mistake about their clothing...
he wears a dress shirt, a loosened tie,
a button fits each buttonhole,
two socks—both dark if not a pair—
shoelaces tied; nothing wrong.

She pins her hair up, two earrings, pierced,
a cotton suit: no crooked seam,
no flaw, nothing neglected or lost.
Neither wears a ring. Maybe
if I try holding the picture away,
at arm's length or upside down...
maybe what's wrong is something said,

a word they pass like salt and pepper
to season any differences....
Still, a dinner shows they're happy,
as happy as possible: that metaphor
for something they imagine others have.
Perhaps what's wrong is finding metaphors
to make a point of distance—or lines
themselves, so neatly drawn—or a mat
that cuts the picture out and says:
Here! Find something wrong!
Or is it how I hold the picture
trying to imagine what it's like?

Story Problem

John and Linda, two bodies in motion,
travel a distance apart within a room
of constant volume, such as a kitchen.
Both possess a given weight: let the sacks
of groceries stand for these. How much work
is done to meet at any point between?

Imagine John and Linda, two bodies
at rest, talking at the kitchen table.
How much work is done if they move from there?
Now imagine a weight they cannot lift,
a tonnage like the stones of pyramids.
(Recall how Egyptians built a road of logs:

as a log rolled free behind, they brought it forward
to bear the weight again.) In this model,
next substitute words for numbers of logs.
Notice how the last thing said is brought up
once more, spoken beneath the moment's weight,
then echoes, a silence that doesn't lift.

How many words are needed for the task?
What if the two have heard it all before:
the dandled hopes, months of planned revisions
that come to mean a promise? Do they forget—
or need forgetting—so they can hear it again?
Time permitting, list other examples.

Recalling the original problem,
a burden they can't lift or bear to leave
behind, the work they've done and have to do,
derive expressions for the following:
a point at rest, a history of travel,
a story where the problem starts or ends.

36

July

We argue over anything:
the nomenclature of a bed of lavenders,
agreeing only Latin names leave well enough alone.
I snap a sample bunch to classify at home
and you pull the rest to fill the centerpiece.
In the car the flowers sway above your hands
the way your head bobs trying to stay awake.
They're nodding *no,* then *yes,* they disagree but settle
(losing petals, limp) when your head meets my shoulder.
The whole way home I want to wake you, I want to say
their loss, their loveliness, it doesn't matter
what Linnaeus called them, how sorry—
I want to slip them through your fingers
and throw them out the window without rousing you
so that the flowers, like dreams we have slept through,
won't be recalled or call us back.

Precipitation

Crossed with rain, crosshatched in the window screen,
the grey is seining all the objects in sight.
The air is sheer as air mail stationery
made thinner from erasure; and what color
is strained, is held afloat, handcolored,
more nearly an afterthought, a moot apology.

So the day is spent (has already been)
listening to rain stop and start and mostly rain,
plotting imponderable degrees in terms
like *downpour, deluge, cats and dogs,* and
    buckets.
Call it *resentment* that floats above the asphalt

mocking us with rainbows: nothing has passed
and rain continues to announce the chance
that nothing will change either. Besides the rain
other objects surface, claiming to be a sentence,
to take the blame like any messenger:

one might as well cause the news as bring it
— were there any news to bear.
But if it's hard to blame anything,
it is, admittedly, hard not to:
the rain, the rainbows, ourselves,

though we are not the summer farmers
delayed eight weeks now, in sowing corn,
haven't their grounds for worry, or losses
we can count on. So what if we drive to work?
We watch the rainfall, irrefutable

as any trivia, chart itself in measurements
we can't convert—I'd say, converse about.
On the TV, colored patterns
crisscross Ohio, boasting of tomorrow:
Showers. Thundershowers, heavy at times...
as though there weren't a chance of holding back.

November

Now without snow the trees seem bare:
there are no leaves and yet the wind
is warm through the window, sluggish
as bees that catch inside your hair.

Something you said perseverates
on the pages though I turn them,
though I look away, staring out
on rain or air about to rain.

I try to phrase what I should say
and then forget it. Already
the room is too dark for reading.
Besides, something might be settled

by someone giving in, turning
on a lamp. Someone does. Between
us the space shows up like a fault
neither overlooks or admits:

it keeps there in the middle.
What can be decided now or
in the morning, for all the leaves
we might expect the trees to bear?

The Same River Twice

Like more leading in the window frame
the branches are quite plainly what we look through:
snow, banks of snow, one riverbank,
a rivulet of river bound in ice—
only an Impressionist's eye might fix
and not lose sight of this. Huge canvases
all vermilion, others maize, then mauve,
he'd paint this same river twice — twenty times,
applying color as though it were, like love,
a subject keen attention could supply.

In bed each of us reads; our books face down,
and open, spread over us like fronds.
And if they offer no real protection
we're neither cold nor lost far from home.
We *are* home, we imagine this home,
though the clock chimes still surprise you
and your warmth distracts me from the distances
I read. How long can we reside this way?
Can I brook that instant when your breath
deepens to sleep, when longing (without object!)
wells inside that smallest difference?

Essentially a love story, what I read
can be applied to our case, to what I know
is not love, but old impatience: this window
where I construe the signs: falling from the eaves,
snow is startling as the edge of the bed;
today's mood is summoned by an overcast sky;
there's an indecision in the narrow sluice
the river concedes at noon, rescinds again
by dinner—if only to insert, "because,"
to tell myself, "coincidence is cause."

What do we look for? A view completely green?
A single story of leaves in a background of leaves
blurred among a few exceptions of blue
that no more convince the eye of distance
than my imagining an artist fills
the empty pane with something picturesque?
Look at the river now. The season will turn
decidedly green—must it be against us?—
obscuring all but two separate memories,
frozen fast, not flowing, bound within lead.

Calling Into Question

Some form of subaudition carries us,
understated, almost misunderstood,
as if love, like a dim star, is best descried
by staring slighly to one side: missing you
informs me I've forgotten you and just remembered;
your scent on my skin blossoms as it showers off.

The rabbis knew nothing was understood:
seeing a friend not seen in months, they praised,
He who revives the dead. Each morning, rising up,
they praised that they could praise that morning.
The world renewed by waking to it,
they knew nothing would hold its place.

Let's say by straying from the subject
(obliquely waddling to the mark in view,
as Pope said) I could mean: *I take it back,*
all the givens, all that's said and done with,
all we never meant or never meant well,
every constellation we described—

Let's say, this once, the past could carry on
without us, and these slanted views could mean:
I don't know, I don't know—such forms of praise.

November, Again

A step behind you in the fog, I watched
your jacket (blue against everything gray)
and thought, beyond this circle our eyes describe,
the field has been erased and only what
we spoke would fix *that* tree, *that* color blue,
in place again. But you were both the window
and the one I wished to call to its view
so I said nothing. For an hour the field
repeated beneath our feet and the fog
kept its distance behind us and in front.
That was November, cold before the snow,
the fog too thick for travel. It's hard still
knowing what I've kept myself from saying.

Freeway Flowers

Postcard

"From Santa Cruz, home, the exits are lined
with what everyone calls *freeway flowers.*
You'd love how in sunlight they burnish
half a hillside pure fool's gold,
the way a cloud will shade the other half
a deep but temporary evergreen.
Littering the parking lots, uprooted
from the redolent freesias and the stands
of calla lillies massed into abstraction,
they argue beauty is more like common sense
than cultivation, that souvenirs
are what you find in place of what you've lost."

Reply from Ohio

Stranded in this uncertain climate
the spindly hibiscus proffers each
of its long-awaited blossoms at arm's length,
a gesture learned from Emily Dickinson:
prepared to brave the worst winds yet
(remember how we'd welcome any draft)
each bears its petals with the resignation
of a brand-new, inside-out umbrella
which must last the day and, eventually,
is dropped along the drenching walk home.

A Second Reply, Never Mailed

Even people who will
to be together, find
that nature begs to differ.
If this is fact, it's proved
only by my wish it were not.
Wrong numbers, clouds,
perennial misgivings,
the any number of neglected things—

an anxious eye finds proof in anything:
There isn't a reason to stay
that isn't a reason to leave.
Thank you for the postcard:
"...the green on the peninsula
is unbelievable anywhere
but in its presence, and what's more,
the hibiscus blooms with an abandon
you could learn to live with..."

December, The Botanical Gardens

What blossoms now blossoms only in name:
the garden is all amaranths: signs
and branches pruned back to battered tines.
Survival here is patience or what's innate.
Tea, cabbage, chinese, each rose that we project
blooms red or pinkish buds or rosy pinked ones
above the wintering brown leaves, still pinioned
and now so scarce, we'd think them worth protection
if they were lovely. There's little else to be seen:
some mallards stored beneath a miniature bridge,
an emerald hothouse nurturing all the privileged—
we're cold, we're missing more than something green.
What blossomed will blossom again, an instinct
left in the early Kingdoms: the child's, the Plant.

COLD SUITOURS

Though private prayer be a brave designe,
Yet publick hath more promises, more love:
And love's a weight to hearts, to eies a signe.
We all are but cold suitours; let us move
    Where it is warmest.

—George Herbert, *The Church-porch*

Our Places at the Table

Through the glass I hear my father
shoveling snowdrifts from our door,
his scraping loud as the nights he snores
and keeps us up. It's snowing harder
but we never help: not my brother
who wants to, nor I, who am older.
We watch how the window cleared of frost
clouds again when mother puffs and taps her
ring on the pane, *Everything's cold! Supper!*
how he clears one step as the one behind is lost.
For a moment blacktop peers through
the fresh snow, slush and ice.
Father keeps shoveling the place
the snow keeps falling into.

The Age When Parents
Don't Need Reasons

It's not the cherries but the time that's ripe.
The tree had made a promise father wouldn't let
the birds break. We hung a dozen pie tins
but the cherries mimicked raindrops on the awnings
and never scared the birds. Neither did father,

clapping beneath the roost at dawn, at dark—
the winter ground where he had scattered feed.
Before they pitted half of every fruit
he coached me up and I dropped them, small and pale,
on sheets tucked at the trunk as if to break a fall.

Mother would stand till dinner crimping shells,
pitting, conceding cups of sugar by teaspoons.
Proud as though the tree were another child
and the pie, something made at school, she served
dessert and father sliced us each a wedge,

an even share of land. Too sweet, too much,
and hard as softened stones—but when we asked
to be excused not a crumb was left
to say we had no manners. Bedtime at nine,
we let him tuck us tight beneath the sheets

like nothing ever happened. He called back
from the stairwell, promising more next week,
red, riper ones. But in our rooms,
my brother, sister, and I were so quiet
it seemed his voice could never reach that high.

50

Vivarium

Wherever we drove you fixed your point,
a folding stool, and like a compass arm
I traced the bank just far as you could see,
uprooting cattails, milkweed; skipping shale
across the lines you watched draw patient zigzags
on the current's moving, not-moving screen.

You taught me how to cast, your body curved
behind, a question mark, rehearsing mine.
The same position held the baseball bat,
golf club; the same unflagging confidence
repeated, "Relax. Swing level. Use your wrist."
Still the fish I caught you had caught first,

reeled close to shore, and called me in to mind
so you could stretch your legs. Without a wait
the line unzipped the water, and as I wound
you scooped the fish up, worked the hook back out
its flashing lip—or worse, its bloody gill.
The stringer grew heavy as an anchor

and moored us there until the day's catch,
stood on end beside me, was taller by a foot.
Before dinner you wrapped them live
inside the Sunday Magazine and wedged the lot
below the fruit bin. Catfish went with the maid.
The rest were cleaned and then delivered to the aunts.

I learned to stay home. You drove farther away.
Some differences were clear: how was I born
blue from your brown eyes, blond from your dark?
Still others took ten years to be expressed:

your weakened heart, my weakened knees, my pieced-
together income, my house without child.

Long distance I learned to recognize
the voice that every day had called your parents
(your buoyancy that couldn't bear much news),
even the spring you phoned from hospitals
when your heartbeat zigzagged on a TV screen
and I watched the line jerk and run with your life.

That scene keeps surfacing like bluegill
at the viviarium, too small for anything
but wishes to toss back in the waves.
The next year or maybe a year later,
bigger and older just as we are,
they meet us at the shallows and take the bait.

Circling Columbus

for Gardner McFall

the world is "manageable" just as you have written.
If I squint, the sound turns visible
beneath the wings—an act of physics made
for believing. I look down while we hover:
each fishery is stocked full of silver coins;
the frozen cornfields ruled like notebook filler
and a silo's tumblerful of winter corn
are one day's work one family has done;
beyond there, arranged along the airport road,
are blocks of hangars and high-rise hotels
with room enough to house us comfortably:
myself and those who make me welcome.

And then we land. The world rises as we expected.
Before we reach the gate they are there,
life-size, Gardner, and even larger.
If love had ever compassed such a scale
(as children looking up, as parents looking ahead),
it must be now, looking back, that makes it so—
the world, "manageable," because we write it so
that moment circling above ground before
anyone has recognized us. They are waiting:
a retriever I left, too excited to pet,
and a younger sister who grabs my luggage because
she's strong enough, then walks straight to the door.

A Family Tree

The night they sprayed the roost you were just five,
supposed to be asleep and the lawn empty
before you woke for school. I planned to lie,
how they flew someplace larger than our elm tree—
like every dog that ran away over
the outerbelt, all to some good family.
It was too dark to tell branches from birds:
the hose struck anywhere. Outlined in foam
a single starling, tree-size, white, appeared.
It wasn't hard to shape the wings from shadows,
to call the quarter moon a beak, up-turned.
The branches disappeared the way warm snow
drops, whole boughs at once. Huddled, undisturbed,
the birds just floated, and when the foam seeped in,
they disappeared. We waited for the birds to drop
with the temperature, to hit the freezing point—
we sprayed again, the weather would decide.
A morning free of frost, the early *Dispatch*
counted fifty-one, which left the same thousands,
our same small flock you always fed your crusts.
You were not asleep though: watching inside
the screen door, a robe beneath your coat;
watching those next days, how the birds fell limp,
(I always imagined) along the streets you crossed
coming from school. I saw their flapping limbs
scooped inside your lunchbox, delivered home
each afternoon like more permission slips,
all asking me: cure them, splint each bone,
provide them shelter until they're airborne,
then set them free. I say it will be all right
as though performing those simple labors
lifted the curse of starlings from our homes.

54

Notes Through the Winter

November 6, 1861

Dear Theresa,
    What news but more of the same? Albert owns
three dozen cages now—and you ask what my day is like?
Can there be metaphors among such likeness? It is noon
or midnight, then, the ostinato of cuckoo-clock
that hoards the hour and will not let it pass. Outside it snows!
but here, the one song is Spring, arriving and arriving:
all the songs are harbingers of nothing more than more song.

    What *is* new, is my lack of forebearance. There was a scene
at supper, and for no reason, unless it was to lie
awake and think of one. Now it's midnight. As I write you
I hear them singing—it is my one continuous dream.
Mine, alone! Father cannot sleep for all his plans to sell,
Albert tends the brood, a mother bird himself (forgive me!),
and Mother folds her words with muslin in her reticule.

    The conversation never strays from birds, it is grace
we say at every meal, the tea that steeps all afternoon.
Albert says, he insists, birds have no feeling in their eyes—
no feelings. He quoted Scripture: how Creation is ours
to finish, inferring a votive charge; that in God's eyes
we may blind God's creatures. I asked why they sing past dark.
Father told how the songbox opens with a key of light,
how it locks again at dusk, and how they throw away the key.
Yet I persisted, asked why is it not forever locked,
and Albert, in tones I need not familiarize you with,
pronounced, "You're not silent, Dear, though you lock
      yourself upstairs."
Theresa, either I have lost all logic in this din,

or I should think that if tomorrow I awakened blind,
I could not feign, nor like the birds forget, I once knew light.

    There was dessert, and Cook—she's new this week—
        had done a torte.
If only that had sated! Instead I tried their patience,
argued how poorly the birds look afterward, battered, dull,
all their feathers bent. At which Albert pointed his teaspoon
to his ear, and his eye, "Less to behold, more to be heard,"
and Father thumped the linen like a Bible, reciting,
"An eye for an eye...." and laughing that he finally gave
the passage purpose, religion, a place at his table.
I could hear no more, and deaf to reason—was I crying?—
shouted, "What is beauty but the eye of the beholder?"
and ran out—crying then, I'm sure—"Blindness for blindness...."

    Misgivings are what we cannot give away, Theresa,
how we ask ourselves forgiveness. If only you could hear
        the birds!
All the songs have changed. They add whistles and rasping
        noises,
droning like a file that wears down the air, flat to the ground
and is itself worn down. I know it is I who have changed,
grown deaf to their song. Now there is no music, no silence:
a rest is still another note, through *I* sound it, more news
of Spring returning to the window ledge, three dozen doves
without one sprig of green. Even letters are no respite
though I send this, add it to the others as Albert adds
new birds. Beneath impertinences that cannot be hidden,
please find the voice of a loving sister, your

                                                Elizabeth

The Fire Pond

We stock the fire pond with rainbows.
I bring home loaves of day-old bread
or else a piece of lung the butcher saved
and Grandfather showers handfuls across the pond
shouting, *There's one! Big as a railroad tie!*
I shout back, *That's longer than my arm!*

The day the Allegheny floods
the rattlers move toward Salamanca and hang
from the elderberries. The trout are spilled
like oil spots down the highway. In June
we stock the pond again. July, Grandfather
sights the smoke rising near the barn.

When the volunteers from Hinsdale rally
he drags the pump hose to the pond and lowers it
like an anchor. The rainbows surface to be fed.
My cousin straps Indian fire pumps on the men
and Grandfather almost saves the corncrib, but when
the sweat steams beneath his rubber coat he falls

and can't get up. Mother sets the horses loose.
To keep the house from catching, one hose
pounds the walls all night. The water pours
down the window, where I watch the embers float,
slow as pennies in a wishing well, from the barn
to the stables, the milk house, and both the silos.

The pond's not deep enough, Grandfather
tells me, as if he'd just remembered how
deep they'd dug it. I forget it's night.
The seven thousand bales blaze till morning,
when the barn frames the sunrise. It's quiet
then, before the firemen coil their hoses

half-filled with sludge, and the crowds drive
home to Portville, Ischua, and Knapp Creek.
Friends in Olean, and farther south
than Hinsdale, smell the smoke at sunup,
the fish at dusk. Grandfather and I
comb the acres after supper. Because nothing stands

but the house and the woods, we watch
the ground as if something were left there
and we had come to look. Across the field
the basin shimmers like a highway in the summer
heat, a still mirage of water, except the silt
ripples where the tails are flaring beneath.

In Exchange for Wood

In a blizzard the neighborhood is closer and farther
apart at once. Windows are drawn with steam
or solid ice. Doors slam on the cold.
Roads close to all but thoughts of travel.

Since the hickory was wider than their house
(its canopy, a good two stories higher),
when I first drove past I thought their house,
not the tree, had been uprooted, felled

by the gale and wedged among the boughs.
It would have been simpler to move a house;
simpler for the two sisters to move away.
We're not their closest neighbors, or close friends

but after a week, no one had touched the tree.
I phoned all seven listings: three weeks
until anyone could come, because of the blizzard,
six hundred dollars plus, because it was hickory.

They couldn't afford to have a switch removed,
let alone replace the shingles, chimney bricks,
glass, furniture—a limb crashed through
the upstairs room that's been for rent two years.

I don't know who is older. I suppose
a person reaches a certain age and is old
and then no older. What's clear is May decided
years ago, Hannah can't decide;

she's aged every other time I visit.
In a few days they phoned to say a man

with an ice-cream truck would remove the tree
in exchange for wood. Of course, they agreed.

The chain broke twice sawing the shaft;
it took six men to roll thirty feet of trunk
against the back fence where it barely fit.
Any wood thinner than a wrist was left.

Some large as trees themselves, the severed limbs
stood askew, embedded in snow like offshoots
the hickory stump was sending from its roots.
Warmer on Saturday and Sunday, as snow

melted, the branches loomed taller and darker.
At night winds flung the lightest limbs
against the house. Piece by piece, the whole
tree fell over and over again in nightmares.

When the winds slackened I cleared their chimney,
started a fire, taught them how to tend
the flames and dry the frozen, still-green wood.
May gathered the kindling closest to the porch —

bundled in layers of sweaters and coats
as though each winter a person grew colder,
required another ring of clothing. I counted
that tree's rings: seventy-some, her age.

I'd say the fire lasted week, ten days
before another call. May was sitting
by the fire, Hannah had dozed off, knitting.
First May thought it was steam from the drying wood;

then she saw the ball of yarn had rolled
to the firescreen and was burning, and the strand
that led to Hannah's dress was burning. She panicked,
seized the afghan, beat the fire out;

the afghan Hannah was knitting to thank me.
Then all her held back tears poured, sudden as rain
after a storm, falling from a shaken tree.
The wood doubled when the snow began to melt.

Starting in March they snapped the limbs they could
(none thicker than a cinnamon stick)
and dragged the widths they couldn't to the fence.
The trashmen only took them bundled,

only two each week, only with a tip.
Ten months: eighty bundles—minus
the weeks of June when Hannah was too sick.
No one's mowed the lawn, raked the leaves

or gardened, though rhubarb shot up in April
and went to seed and in June, strawberries
and hyacinths rotted beneath the trunk.
Linen swaths, ribbons—one time the faggots

were bound with scraps, knotted end to end,
like someone scraping together every penny
he can find (from cluttered drawers, pockets
of summer clothes) to meet a weekly debt.

Judging from the yard, this is their life's work:
two bundles each week, carefully wrapped
like heirlooms for a distant relative.
Once they have parted with the precious things,

the letters, generations of picture frames
and jars, what could remain for anyone
to take, but the house (which someone will)
and their lives, which is all they've left to decide?

Driving Past Morocco, Indiana

Somebody else can love this flattened land,
the someone that is my husband, or the child
we wish for more than rain, when all we see
are dust clouds; or when the sprouts wash onto the drive,
their bowed heads above their two leaves
praying, more than we wish the rain would stop.
The preacher tells us wishing overlooks
what love would be able to see. Well, someone else
will have to love ten thousand perfect furrows,
plowed in the one direction: away. Wherever
you look they lead your eyes away, the rows
becoming one, like our voices in church—
swelling and never coming back—as though
all a man has to do is sow
a straight line from his house, through his fields
and eventually he reaches heaven.

If I were a child, I'd stand in the living room
(where we have one view in our four windows)
close my eyes and spin until I'm dizzy
and lose direction. Then I'd quick look
and say which window I'm seeing through:
true, early corn is higher out the north;
and it's true, shade wanders in from the west field,
cuts through the hedge of floribundas,
stays for lunch and leaves out the back,
the same familiar stranger every day.
If it's been traveling longer than we've stayed put,
what does that make us? Newer strangers?

I'm not forgetting we do have neighbors (none
in shouting range) and a phone (you don't need
to shout into that) and relatives to write
and a freeway that's always disguised
(like our temptations) with fog or snow or corn—
except for holidays, when the families

drive past like they don't even see our house.
Or like they do, whichever's faster.
But it's no temptation. We take that road to church.

Before the phone was in, there was no one but me.
During the storms I'd stare at the crab apple
by the bedroom and think, I'm the only one
who will hear it fall and it's the only one
—and it won't even hear—if I fall. There's a tree
outside the nursery, more on the side
that faces Mr. Chandler's, who wouldn't hear
if you shouted *help* straight at his ear.

In the rain everything's turned a shade
of hay turning to straw turning to compost.
After our porch, the lawn becomes the field,
and it becomes Mr. Chandler's field
and then his lawn, then Morocco, and more
Indiana, where someone might be wishing
these clouds to do just the opposite.
It's dizzying to think what God must see.

All I can see is how rain has filled
every furrow to the brim and how
—if I keep watching—it pools into one spill,
spilling like a full waterglass
someone just knocked to the kitchen floor.
If I close my eyes, there's a mother wishing
her child hadn't broken the glass, and a fence
where there's a father sawing planks for where
a car must have swerved in the pouring rain.
When he's sure the fence will hold, he walks
in through the fields, the floribundas,
into the kitchen, eats supper and so on.
No one mentions the water or the child.
Over the years they've learned: when the husband says
horizon, I understand, *the world curves.*

Strand

Whether we quicken our steps
pretending a destination,
or drag our feet, pretending none,
the shorebirds pace with us
an unnegotiable distance ahead.
At least, their shadows do,
and their zigzagging trails.

As one wave rolls to shore,
unrolls over the sand, then retreats,
the stranded water suggests
a continent, a western coast,
peninsulas and bays—
uncharted as something remembered.
It spreads open across the beach's

lap, the flock of shadows dash
to settle it and set up shop,
and except for the cross-stitched tracks,
overlapping and then intersecting
our own more weighty version,
the place is all but
forgotten among the sands.

Another wave revises
its dark ink in a deckled seaboard:
it's our turn to orient ourselves
in the oceans of sand—or so they seem.
That star's reflection...
is the capital of what? What island
is this sinking tidal pool?

Such dim unwieldly geography!
Was it here! Could it have been here?
asks each arriving map.
What's certain is we won't catch

up with the birds (who've had
no easier time trying to pin down
that hem of surf: as fast as one seam

is fixed in place, the incoming tide
unfastens it). *We're* through pretending.
We leave the birds their drastic—
more likely, temporary–measures
and turn back toward the strand
of new hotels. But now the eastern

coasts unroll and roll, or ravel,
unravel: *Here! No? Well, where then?*

65

PRINCETON SERIES OF CONTEMPORARY POETS

Library of Congress Cataloging in Publication Data

Rosen, Michael J., 1954-
   A drink at the mirage.

   (Princeton series of contemporary poets)
   I. Title.   II. Series.
PS3568.O769D7   1984   811'.54   84-15016
ISBN 0-691-06627-2
ISBN 0-691-01417-5 (pbk.)